CONTENTS

KU-432-989

Alan & Brenda Stockwell are directors of The Stockwell Puppet Theatre, Vesper Cottage, Smarden, Ashford, Kent, an educational project which visits primary schools throughout the country with a programme of dramatised folk tales.

They also give lecture-demonstrations on puppet making to teachers.

Easy-to-make
PUPPETS

by ALAN and BRENDA STOCKWELL
with illustrations by
ERIC WINTER

Publishers: Ladybird Books Ltd . Loughborough
© Ladybird Books Ltd 1973
Printed in England

Introduction

It is fun to give a puppet-show and this book will tell you how to do it.

We start by telling you how to make the simplest kinds which are flat, finger puppets made from cardboard. Then we pass on to more advanced forms and also suggest some ideas for stages and plays.

All the puppets can be quickly and easily made, and most of the materials required will be found around the house.

For colouring the puppets, poster paints are best although the cardboard ones can be coloured easily with felt-tip pens.

You need not restrict your characters to the ones we have made. These methods can be used for all kinds of different characters.

0 7214 0349 2

An elephant finger puppet

You will need :

Thin card (a postcard will do)
Paints or crayons

Draw the outline of an elephant similar to the diagram below. Cut it out. Cut a hole as shown, big enough to take the first finger. Your finger is the elephant's trunk !

Colour the elephant.

If you wish you can also paint your finger to match the elephant's body.

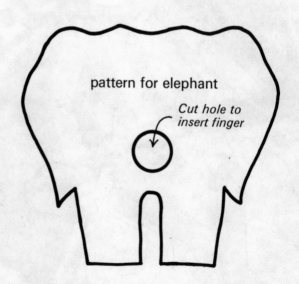

pattern for elephant

Cut hole to insert finger

A puppet with finger legs

You will need:

Thin card (postcards will do)
Cotton wool
Glue
Paints or crayons
Stiff paper

Draw the outline of Santa Claus as shown in the little diagram on the opposite page but making it about 5″ (127mm) high. Cut it out. Cut two holes near the bottom of the body. These holes are for your first and second fingers.

Colour the body red and the belt black. You can stick on cotton wool for his beard and whiskers and for the trimming of his hat and tunic.

For his boots, roll two tubes of stiff paper to fit on the fingers (A) and cut four foot shapes as (B). Glue the foot shapes to the tubes. When the glue is dry, colour the boots red and black.

You will have made a Father Christmas but you could make some different people in just the same way.

Cut two holes to insert fingers.

For boots, make cylinder of stiff paper to fit finger.

A

Cut two shapes for each foot and glue together at shaded portion.

B

Pinch together lower end of cylinder A and slide portion B upwards and glue firmly to sides.

A

B

A paper-bag puppet

You will need :

A paper bag
Paints, crayons or felt-tip pens

Fold back the bottom corners of the bag and glue behind as shown in the small diagram below.

Paint a figure on the front of the bag. Cut two holes at the front for your fingers.

You work the puppet with your hand inside the bag. Your first finger sticks up into the top of the bag and your thumb and second finger poke through the holes to make the puppet's arms. Your other two fingers are bent out of the way into the palm of the hand, as shown in the small diagram on page 41.

Bottom of bag

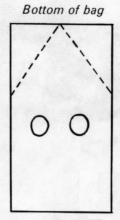

A flat mask head

You will need:

> Postcards
> Glue
> Paints, crayons or felt-tip pens

Draw and paint and cut out a face. In the picture opposite are a Red Indian, a Witch and a Pig. The faces can be of any person or animal you wish.

For the neck, roll a piece of card into a tube and glue it onto the back of the mask. Or instead of a tube you can make a simple cardboard tab which you glue on the back. Both ways are shown in the three small diagrams.

For the body of this type of puppet you can use the one shown on page 25.

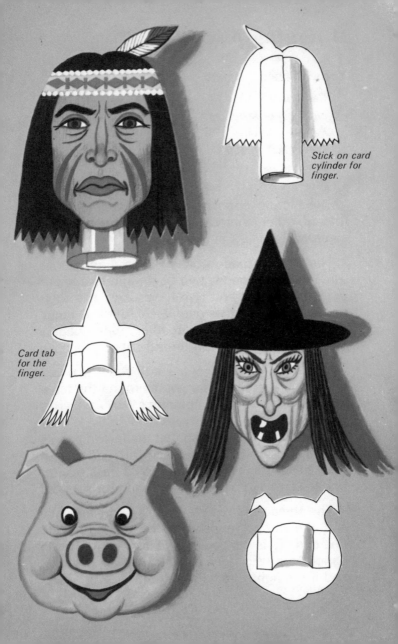

Stick on card cylinder for finger.

Card tab for the finger.

A jigging puppet

You will need:

> Cardboard
> Eight paper-fasteners
> Paints
> Long black thread
> Drawing pin

The picture opposite shows a skeleton, but lots of other characters can be made in the same way.

The body is made from cardboard and is cut out in separate parts: two upper and two lower arms, two upper and two lower legs, and then the head and trunk as one piece. All these limbs are fastened loosely together with paper-fasteners. Make sure the limbs pivot very loosely.

One end of a length of black thread is tied to a table leg. The other end passes round the table leg nearest to the manipulator's hand which is some distance away. Hook the body of the puppet over the thread so that the thread passes across the front of the body and underneath each of the arms. The string could pass over or under a drawing pin in the table leg for support.

The thread is invisible from a short distance and the puppet appears to be dancing quite unaided. It is particularly realistic if made to dance to music from a record player or radio, and if the light is not too bright.

Manipulator can move to a greater or lesser distance from puppet as required for effect.

audience

A jumping jack

You will need :

Cardboard
Eight paper-fasteners
Thread
Cork
A thin stick
Paints

The body is made from separate cardboard parts : head and trunk in one part, two upper arms, two lower arms, two upper legs, two lower legs. The parts should be painted before assembling them with paper-fasteners. Make sure the limbs pivot very loosely.

Join the tops of the arms together with a short slack thread. Join the tops of the legs together with another short slack thread. Connect the two short lengths together with a long thread which hangs down below the puppet. When the thread is pulled the limbs shoot out.

Glue a cork behind the head and push a thin stick into the cork. You can hold the stick in one hand and pull the thread with the other.

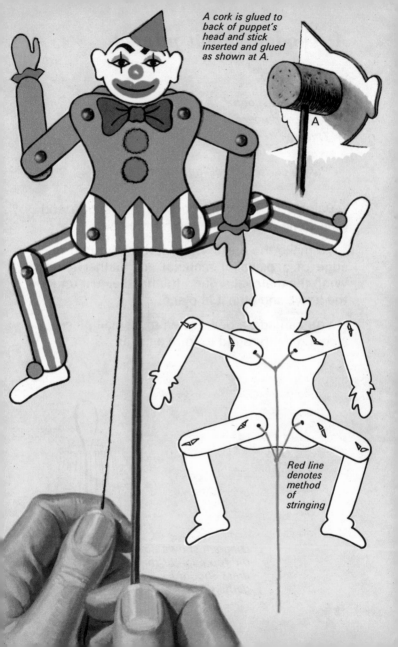

A cork is glued to back of puppet's head and stick inserted and glued as shown at A.

Red line denotes method of stringing

A wooden spoon puppet

You will need:

A wooden spoon
A piece of material
Thread
Wool
Paints, crayons or felt-tip pens

Paint a face on the back of the spoon and glue some wool on the top for the hair.

To make the dress, run a thread through one edge of a piece of material and gather it up. Wrap the material around the handle, just under the bowl, and glue it in place.

You can add a bow, or wrap a small piece of lace trimming round to form a collar.

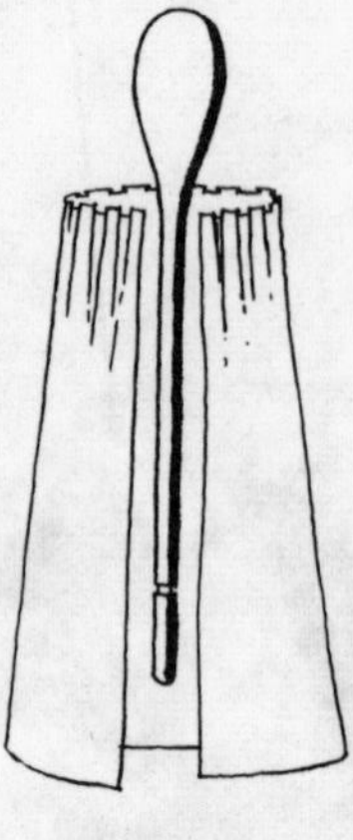

Diagram shows how the top edge of the dress should be gathered

A talking matchbox head

You will need:

A matchbox (the household size is best)
Gumstrip or 'Sellotape'
Thin card (a postcard)
Cotton wool
A piece of red felt
Paints or crayons
A strip of white paper

Take the tray out of the matchbox.

Cut away a third of the front cover (A). Using gumstrip, stick the offcut across the lower part of the open side of the tray (C).

In the tray, cut a round finger hole in the position shown (D). In the back of the cover cut a long slot the same width as the finger hole.

To make the inside of the mouth, cut and fold a strip of white paper the same width as the tray. *After drawing the teeth, attach to tray as shown on diagram (C).

Use thin card to cover up printed fronts of matchbox and the portion attached to tray.

Put tray back into cover.

Draw a mouth with the top lip on the cover and the bottom lip on the offcut. Draw a face and add whiskers, eyebrows and hair, using cotton wool. Cut a hat shape from felt and glue it on the front at the top of the box.

Draw, cut out and paint a body from card and glue it on the back of the box just below the long slot.

*Some household matchboxes have a divider in the tray and the teeth can be drawn on this.

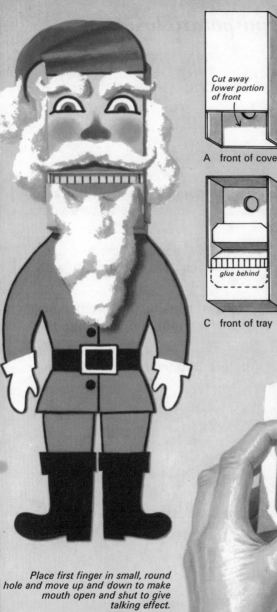

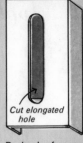

A   front of cover

Cut away lower portion of front

B   back of cover

Cut elongated hole

C   front of tray

glue behind

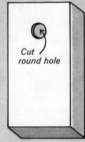

D   back of tray

Cut round hole

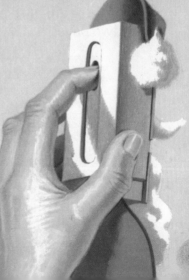

Place first finger in small, round hole and move up and down to make mouth open and shut to give talking effect.

Apple and potato heads

You will need:

An apple or potato
Drawing pins
A felt-tip pen
Two coins

Take out some of the core from the apple with a knife or apple-corer. If you use a potato, you will need to cut a similar hole to take your first finger.

For eyes you can use drawing pins or pieces of black felt. Or you can mark them on with a felt-tip pen.

Ears can be coins of suitable size or cut from cardboard and pushed into the apple at the right places.

The body for this puppet is shown on the next two pages.

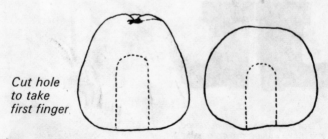

Cut hole
to take
first finger

A body for apple head and flat masks

You will need:

A handkerchief
Two rubber bands

Hold your hand as shown in the drawing below. Drape the handkerchief over the hand.

Wedge the apple or potato onto the first finger. Put rubber bands over the thumb and second finger, to make the puppet's moveable arms.

This body can be used for the masks on page 12.

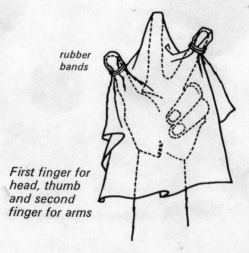

rubber bands

First finger for head, thumb and second finger for arms

A simple rod puppet

You will need:

A stick
An old stocking
A piece of material
Thread
Padding (cotton wool or old rags)
Wool
Scraps of material

Wrap some padding round the top of the stick to make a ball shape and pull the stocking over it. Tie thread round the stick to hold the head in place.

Glue wool on top of the head for the hair. Cut out eyes and mouth from scraps of material and stick in place.

For the body – run a thread through one edge of a piece of material and gather it up. Wrap it around the stick and glue in position.

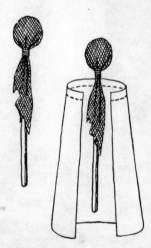

A rod puppet witch

You will need:

A ball	Green wool
Wire	Elastic thread
A stick	Black material
Gumstrip	Yellow and black paint
Cardboard	Paper

Make a hole in the ball and glue it on the stick. Cut two shapes out of the black material as shown in the small diagram opposite. Sew or glue the shapes together round all the edges except the bottom.

Put the stick through a hole at the neck of the body and glue the material to the ball and stick. Sew or glue into the shoulders two pieces of wire or thin wood as (B).

Make the hands by twisting five short pieces of wire together and covering with gumstrip. For the hat copy the patterns below, making the brim from card and the cone from paper. Glue the hands in the ends of the sleeves as (C). Paint the hands and head yellow and add a face. Glue the green wool hair into position before you glue on the hat.

Attach fine elastic from a finger of each hand through the hat brim and down to the shoulder as (A). This gives the effect of free movement of the hands when the rod is twisted.

Patterns for cone and brim of hat

glue

A dog puppet

You will need :

An empty washing-up liquid tube
Thick wool (rug wool is ideal)
Two 12" (305mm) sticks
Black paint or a felt-tip pen

Cut the wool into short strands and glue along the tube, allowing the wool to fall on either side.

Paint two black eyes on the spout end.

Make two small holes to take the sticks as shown.

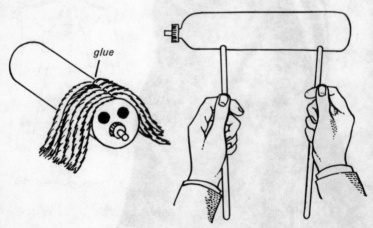

glue

insert two 12" (305mm) sticks

A caterpillar puppet

You will need:

> Coloured paper cut into pieces 6" (152mm) ×2" (51mm)
> A table-tennis ball
> A small piece of dowel
> Two sticks
> Black paper

Lay one piece of paper (A) across the centre of another (B) in the shape of a cross. Bend (A) loosely round (B) and glue the ends to the back of (B). Lay another piece across the back of (A) and in the same direction. Glue the ends of (B) to this strip.

Carry on like this until the caterpillar's body is long enough. You will need at least twenty pairs of papers. You will have made a sort of compressed paper-chain.

Paint a table-tennis ball pink, and stick on eyes and mouth cut from black paper. Make a nose by glueing a small piece of dowel in place.

Make a hat out of black paper and glue onto the ball. Glue the head to one end of the body. Glue a stick at both ends, putting them in the end links.

A

B

B *glue*

A

side view

B

A

A flowerpot puppet

You will need :

A yogurt tub or plastic flowerpot
A stick
A table-tennis ball
A piece of material
A piece of wallpaper
Pink felt for the hands
Wool for the hair
Feather and felt for the hat

Paint a face on the ball and make a hole at the neck. Push the stick into the hole and glue in position (Fig. 1). Glue wool in place for hair and make a hat from a disc of felt and a feather. Glue in place as Figs. 2 and 3.

Glue the piece of material around the inside of the rim of the yogurt tub (Fig. 4). Make a hole in the middle of the bottom of the tub and push the stick down through it.

Gather up the top of the material with a running thread and wrap around the stick. Glue the gathering to the stick and the ball (Fig. 5).

Cut two mitten shapes from felt and glue on to the cloth body as hands.

Decorate the tub by glueing a piece of wallpaper around it. The puppet bobs up and down as you push and pull the stick, and turns as you twist the stick (Fig. 6).

fig. 1   glue

fig. 2   glue

fig. 3   glue

fig. 4   glue

fig. 5   glue

fig. 6

A simple glove puppet head

You will need:

Postcards
Paints
A scrap of fur or wool

Roll one postcard into a tube to make the head (A) and glue the ends together. Roll another postcard into a smaller tube for the neck (B) large enough to fit the first finger. Glue tube (B) firmly inside tube (A) so that about 1″ (25mm) sticks out.

Paint the large tube to look like a face, and over the open top glue a hank of wool or a piece of fur. For the puppet illustrated opposite, silver-grey, long nylon fur was used for the hair.

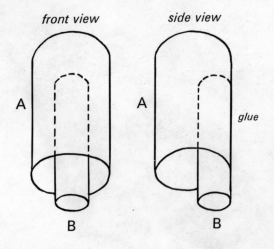

front view   *side view*

A   A

glue

B   B

A papier mâché head

You will need :

Some instant papier mâché
Cardboard 4" (102mm) × 12" (305mm)
Strip of foam sponge rubber about 2" (51mm) wide
Paints

Roll the cardboard into a tube, or use the core of a toilet roll (A).

Wrap the strip of sponge around the tube towards one end, and glue in place (B).

Mix up some papier mâché and cover the sponge, making a ball shape (C). Model the features clearly. Do not forget the ears on the side of the head (D). You will need only a thin layer of papier mâché at the neck end of the tube.

When the modelling is finished, the head must be left to dry. You will have to be patient as drying may take several days. When dry, paint the head.

We have made a Harlequin head but, of course, you can make all sorts of characters.

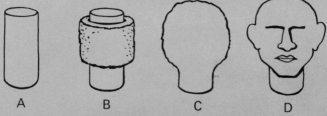

A B C D

A glove puppet body

You will need :

A piece of material
Thin card (postcards are good)
A needle and cotton
Pink paint for the hands

Fold the material in two with the right side inside. Lay your hand on it in the position shown in the small drawing on the opposite page. Draw round your hand, allowing plenty of space all round. Especially make sure you have made it wide enough at the part marked X – X on the drawing.

Cut out the shape. You now have two shirt shapes which must be sewn together up each side and along the top. Leave the shirt open at the bottom, cuffs and neck. Turn inside out so the right side is now outermost.

For the hands, roll cardboard tubes as (A). One is to fit the thumb, the other to fit the second finger. Glue inside one end, pinch together, and cut to shape as indicated at (B). Paint pink. Glue the hands into the cuff openings, and the head (the ones on pages 36/37 or 38/39) into the neck opening.

X   X

A   B

Method of making
hands

Improvised stages

Whilst a proper puppet stage is very nice, you can put on a good show without one. A suitable stage can be made quite simply from things found around the house. Some ideas are shown on the opposite page :

(A) shows two chairs placed back to back at a distance, with a pole resting across them. A curtain is draped over or pinned to the pole.

(B) shows a curtain pinned across an open doorway.

(C) shows a clothes-line stretched between two points, with a sheet draped over. It can be pegged at the ends to stop it from slipping.

(D) is a clothes-horse with wallpaper pinned over it.

All these stages are used as shown in Fig. E. If the stage is placed about 2′ (610mm) in front of the wall of the room, scenery can be drawn on a sheet of paper and pinned to the wall.

A glove puppet booth

An older person could help you with this.

You need six wooden frames made from suitable lengths of 2″ (51mm) × 1″ (25mm) wood as shown in Fig. 1. These are hinged together as shown with ten 2″ (51mm) hinges. Note especially that the two hinges joining the centre large frames are on one side (front) and all the other hinges are on the other side of the frames. This enables the sides to fold in behind and then the whole thing folds forward in half. Thus when folded the booth is the size of one large frame and four frames thick (i.e., 4″ (102mm)).

The frames are covered individually on the outside with cloth tacked in place as shown in Fig. 2, leaving the larger upper one uncovered.

Note the holes which should be made through the side frames. These are to take metal skewers or knitting needles to keep the frames safely together.

Two notches are made on the top of the side frames near the back. These take a rod from which a painted scene (Figs. 3 and 4) can hang. Alternatively a piece of curtaining can form a backcloth.

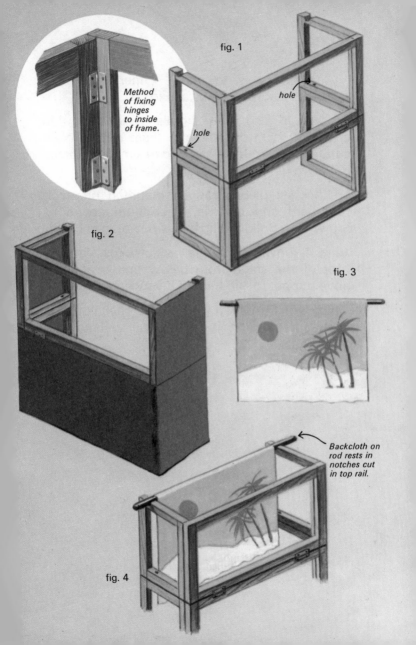

Method of fixing hinges to inside of frame.

fig. 1

hole

hole

fig. 2

fig. 3

fig. 4

Backcloth on rod rests in notches cut in top rail.

Scenery

A simple way to make scenery is to cut pictures from magazines as Fig. 1.

You can also draw simple designs on thin card, cut them out and pin them onto a plain curtain background. This kind of simple set piece is shown in Fig. 2.

Other set pieces can be mounted on thick cardboard and held in place from above or below with Bulldog clips. This is shown in Fig. 3.

Fig. 4 shows an armchair which clips onto the front of the stage from below and enables a glove puppet to 'sit' behind it very convincingly.

Why not try painting an entire backcloth on paper and pinning it to the wall behind the stage ?

fig. 1

fig. 2

fig. 3

fig. 4

'Props'

'Props' is a theatre word which means properties – all the loose things which the players handle and use.

All kinds of props can be made by using a little ingenuity. Our picture shows various props which can be made quite easily.

A simple cardboard box with a lid that can be raised.

A cloth bag filled with washers.

A flowerpot made from a yogurt tub with a paper flower on a wire stem.

A goblet which is a wooden egg cup painted with gilt paint.

Props can also be attached to the puppets' hands like the bucket and the miniature bottle shown in the illustration. The bucket is made from a yogurt tub with a wire handle.

Glove puppets are good at picking things up and handling props but a wide ledge to the front of the stage opening is essential. A length of wood 4″ (102mm) × $\frac{5}{8}$″ (16mm) is ideal.

Types of play

When you have made several puppets you will probably want to act a play with them.

You can make up a simple play by starting with one character (say a dog) then having a second character enter (this could be a witch). Make up a conversation between them. Then add a third person (perhaps Santa Claus) and soon you will find a story developing.

For example: A dog is playing. A witch appears and tries to persuade the dog to go with her. He won't go so she steals him, and hides. Santa Claus enters with a present for the witch. When she comes out for it the dog runs away.

Another way is to adapt a folk tale or nursery rhyme and make puppets for the characters in the story.

A third type of play is a mime. You play a record and the puppets mime to the music. Our picture shows a story where various witches and ghosts try to frighten a boy without success. In the end the boy frightens them away by stretching his head in the air! The music is 'Danse Macabre' by Saint-Saëns.

Some materials you will need to make your puppets

Thin card (postcards)
Paints, felt-tip pens or crayons
Cotton wool
Glue
A paper bag
Brass paper-fasteners
Needle and cotton
A cork
Thin sticks
A wooden spoon
Scraps of material
Wool
A matchbox (household size)
Gumstrip or 'Sellotape'
Coloured felt
White and black paper
An apple or potato
Drawing pins
Two coins
A handkerchief
Rubber bands
An old stocking
A small ball
Wire
Elastic thread
An empty washing-up
   liquid tube
Rug wool
Table-tennis balls
A yogurt tub or plastic
   flowerpot
Wallpaper
A feather
Scraps of fur
Papier mâché
Foam sponge rubber
A pair of scissors

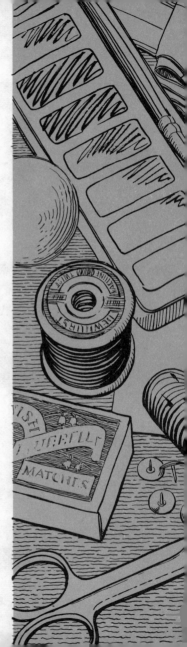